CONTENTS

Front cover: *Gilded Bone China statue of George Washington. ca. 1880. Height 8 1/4 inches (21 cm.). Imprinted Wedgwood, Portland Vase trademark.*

WEDGWOOD AND AMERICA

WEDGWOOD BAS-RELIEF WARE

by David Buten and Patricia Pelehach

Monographs in Wedgwood Studies, Nos. 1 & 2

THE BUTEN MUSEUM OF WEDGWOOD 1977

PREFACE

WEDGWOOD collectors are fortunate in that a comparatively large number of factory records, documents, pattern books, and sales orders are still in existence. Much of this information has been deposited in the University of Keele (England) archives, and is now undergoing cataloguing and microfilming in order that this valuable resource be preserved for years to come. As more and more information is analyzed and published, we increase our understanding of Wedgwood ceramics and of the artists and businessmen, the Wedgwood family in particular, who contributed to the company's success.

One of the purposes of the Buten Museum of Wedgwood is to provide collectors with the information essential to collecting and appreciating Wedgwood ware. In an effort to do this on a regular basis, the *BMW Bulletin* is published seven to nine times per year, and includes short articles on specific subjects. For subjects which require a more extensive format, we are introducing the Buten Museum of Wedgwood *Monographs in Wedgwood Studies.* This first volume contains Monographs Nos. 1 and 2, bound together in a single book. It is hoped that this new publication of the Buten Museum will be a source of information and inspiration for all students of Wedgwood.

We wish to acknowledge the assistance of Temple University's American Studies Program; with the support of the National Endowment of Humanities, two Temple students, Grace Sedberry and Lorraine Verderame, were able to do the initial research for the Buten Museum's Bicentennial exhibition, *Wedgwood and America.* Special assistance in mounting the exhibition was given by Gail Stern, Coordinator of Field Work for the American Studies Program at Temple. We would also like to thank those who loaned pieces for the exhibition: Mr. Milton Aion, Mrs. John Boyko, Mr. and Mrs. Samuel Laver, Mr. and Mrs. S. Arthur Levy, Mr. Theodore Miller, Mrs. Seal Simons-Newmark and Independence National Historical Park. Except where noted, all pieces illustrated are from the collection of the Buten Museum of Wedgwood.

Lastly, we would like to thank all the members of the Buten Museum without whose interest and support this volume would not exist. We hope that you will enjoy this addition to the literature about Wedgwood.

David Buten, F.R.S.A., *Director*
Patricia Pelehach, *Assistant to the Director*

WEDGWOOD AND AMERICA

by David Buten and Patricia Pelehach

Monographs in Wedgwood Studies, No. 1

INTRODUCTION: JOSIAH WEDGWOOD'S SUPPORT OF THE AMERICAN REVOLUTION

JOSIAH Wedgwood's sympathy with the aims and ideals of the American colonists during the Revolutionary War is well documented in his letters to his friend and business partner, Thomas Bentley. As "Potter to the Queen," Wedgwood often found it expedient to play down his pro-American sentiments, but he shared his feelings freely with Bentley and other friends. Well before open warfare broke out between England and America, Wedgwood predicted that Britain's policy toward her North American colonies would lead to disastrous results. In May of 1761 Wedgwood wrote to Bentley:

> Mr. Granville and his party seem determin'd to Conquer England in America I believe. If the Americans do not comply with their demands respecting the quartering of soldiers, the alternative, I am told, is to be, the suspension of the Legislative power in America. I tell them the Americans will then make laws for themselves and if we continue our Policy—for us too in a very short time. But I have very little time at present to bestow upon Politicks, if we must all be driven to America, you and I shall do very well amongst the Cherokee Vid—the Basketmaker.[1]

A few days later he wrote again to Bentley saying:

> I was with Mr. Bagot this morning and we had a good deal of chat upon political affairs, particularly American, in which I told him my sentiments very freely. That our Policy had a tendency to render the Americans independent a century sooner than they would be in the common order of events, if treated agreeable to sound policy.[2]

One might wonder how a man like Wedgwood, with his particular background and social position, could hold such liberal (and, at that time, unpopular) views.

In order to understand the ideas and circumstances that molded Wedgwood's political outlook, one must examine the changes in English society during the Industrial Revolution (1760-1840). According to historian Steven A. Shapin, the Industrial Revolution "produced not only a new economic order, it also produced a new culture. Ideas of progress, of rationality, and above all, of utility permeated the rapidly growing new manufacturing towns of provincial Britain and attracted many of their literate classes to an unprecedented participation in culture." Shapin argues that "science was an integral part of a class self-image," and that it played a significant cultural role in British society.[3] He goes on to explain that the study of natural science and the rise of clubs and societies devoted to this study were among the "characteristic forums of this participation."

The most celebrated of the provincial scientific societies was the Lunar Society of Birmingham, an informal group of intellectual, energetic, and forward-looking men who were committed to rational, scientific, liberal ideals. The Society, founded in 1768, included in its membership James Watt, Erasmus Darwin and Joseph Priestley. Since Josiah Wedgwood lived some distance away from Birmingham, he was not a regular member of the meetings, but he did occasionally attend the Society's lectures and he kept in touch with the other members. Thus, he was in contact with some of the most innovative and progressive thinkers and experimenters of his day. Wedgwood fit in easily with the members of the Lunar Society, and he found their attitudes congenial with his own.

While he was yet a partner with Thomas Whieldon, Wedgwood had begun controlled, recorded experiments upon ceramics. He wrote this description about the process:

> This suite of experiments was begun at Fenton Hall, in the parish of Stoke upon Trent, about the beginning of the year, 1759, in my partnership with Mr. Whieldon, for the improvement of our manufacture of earthen ware, which at that time stood in great need of it, the demands for our goods decreasing daily, and the trade universally complained of as being bad & in a declining condition . . . I had already made an imitation of Agate: which was esteemed beautiful & a considerable improvement: but people were surfeited with wares of these variegated colours. These considerations induced me to try for some more solid improvement, as well in the *Body*, as the *Glazes*, the *Colour*, & the *Forms* of the articles of our manufacture.[4]

Wedgwood was extremely interested in the application of scientific observation and methods to the production of ceramics. At this time, pot-making was still very much a small cottage industry; however, in the next few decades it was to expand into a full-fledged factory system. This metamorphosis was, to a great extent, dependent upon the new methods and improvements introduced by Josiah Wedgwood. Wedgwood's talent for scientific experimentation did not go unnoticed by his contemporaries; he was elected a Friend of the Royal Society for his work on the pyrometer, a device he invented for measuring the extremely high temperatures of the pottery kilns.

It is important to note, as Steven Shapin points out in his article, that the tangible successes and scientific discoveries encouraged by the provincial scientific societies are much less important historically than the less apparent, but fundamentally more significant, social changes they heralded and promoted. Science gave form to a philosophy that was essentially "progressive, anti-authoritarian, egalitarian, empirical, down-to-earth, and common-sensical;" however, the middle class professional men who comprised the societies guarded against the social excesses of unchecked democracy, by continually reaffirming the virtues of respectability, order, and Christian morality. Thus, the societies served to establish essential democratic ideals while at the same time clearly separating their serious, educated, talented members from the disagreeable, illiterate lower classes.

Given this particular intellectual climate in the provinces, Josiah Wedgwood's pro-American sentiments seem somewhat less surprising. It is important to note that these sentiments were apparently very deeply felt; Wedgwood continued to speak up in favor of American independence even when the war ended his lucrative trade with the colonies. He was quite exasperated with what he regarded as shortsighted and narrow-minded attitudes on the part of British political leaders and the general public. On January 8, 1775 he wrote to Bentley:

> I am no Polititian—All the World are with the Ministers & against the poor Americans —They are all gone' mad & I have given them up for incurables.[5]

On February 6, 1775, he wrote again:

> I do not know how it happens, but a general infatuation seems to be gone forth, & the poor Americans are deemed Rebeles, now the Minister has declared them so, by a very great majority wherever I go.[6]

Although Wedgwood freely expressed his opinions to Bentley, he was not anxious to be publicly identified with the American cause. Thus, although he contributed money to a fund for the relief of American captives in Britain, he wished to remain anonymous. He wrote to Bentley twice concerning this, on December 22 and December 29, 1777.

> You may subscribe 10 or £20, or what you please for me towards alleviating the miseries of the poor captives, under the signature of A B C or what you please. Gratitude to their countrymen for their humanity to G. Burgoine & his army is no small motive for my mite.[7]

> * * * * *

> I have more reasons than one why my name should not appear in the list, which I will tell you when I have the pleasure of seeing you, but in the mean time be so good to subscribe 10 guineas for me, or double that sum if you think proper, because I think it is a charity that should not be postpon'd, & if you afterwards convince me that I ought to give my name, I will do it along with two or three guineas more, which is as much as I would put my name to, if I did it now.[8]

Bentley, from his vantage point in London, continued to keep Wedgwood informed on the course of the war. In his replies, it is evident that although Wedgwood was pleased to learn of American victories, he was concerned that the British would sustain severe losses.

> I . . . bless'd my stars and Ld North that America was free. I rejoice most sincerely that it is so, & the pleasing ideas of a refuge being provided for those who chuse rather to flee from than submit to the iron hand of tyrany has raised so much hilarity in my mind that I do not at present feel for our own situation as I may do the next rainy day. We must have more war, & perhaps continue to be beat—to what degree is in the womb of time. If our drubbing keeps pace with our deserts, the L^d have mercy upon us.[9]

Upon finally hearing from Bentley about peace at last in America, Wedgwood's first reaction was disbelief. This letter is particularly interesting because it shows that Bentley had access to important political information that had not yet appeared in the newspapers.

> I had almost given up the account of the flag of truce from America, & my principal reason was because I thought it too good to be true, & not because our governors had not published it in any of the prints, well knowing they hold the people too cheap to think it worth while to publish anything merely for their information; but as your authority for the fact appears so good to you, I do not yet give it up.[10]

Wedgwood was very glad to hear about prospects for peace in America; he approved of the establishment of a free and democratic United States, and looked forward to the resumption of trade with the new nation. The importance of America as a market for Wedgwood's wares is discussed in the next chapter.

USEFUL WARE: THE FOUNDATION
OF WEDGWOOD'S TRADE

WHEN Wedgwood first set up as an independent potter in 1759, the pottery trade between England and her American colonies was already well established.[11] Typical Staffordshire ceramic products such as agate, tortoise shell, cauliflower, pineapple, and "engin'd" red ware were all popular in America before the Revolution. Agate and tortoise were named after the natural materials they were intended to resemble. Cauliflower and pineapple were elaborate naturalistic shapes produced as teapots, tea caddies, and similar pieces. "Engin'd" red ware was made from a common dark red body and decorated with attractive geometric designs produced with the use of an engine-turned lathe.

Queen's Ware gravy boat with fixed stand and artichoke finial. Hand-painted decoration in orange and black. This piece is typical of the kind of ware Wedgwood was exporting to America before the Revolution. ca. 1780. Height 6½ inches (15.8 cm.). Impressed Wedgwood, M.

By 1763 Wedgwood, too, was shipping his ceramic wares to North America.[12] In addition to the traditional wares, Wedgwood shipped examples of his attractive, inexpensive, cream-colored ware (Queen's Ware), which was to form the basis for his financial success. This fine, lightweight body, which was in production by 1761, consisted of ground flint plus pipeclay covered with an improved lead glaze which resisted cracking or "crazing." Wedgwood described it as "a species of earthenware for the table quite new in its appearance, covered with a rich and brilliant glaze bearing sudden alternations of heat and cold, manufactured with ease and expedition, and consequently cheap having every requisite for the purpose intended."[13]

Wedgwood's fine cream-colored ware got its name, Queen's Ware, in 1766-67. In June of 1765 Wedgwood received an order, through Miss Deborah Chetwynd, for a tea set for Queen Charlotte, wife of George III. The pieces were to be made "with a gold ground and raised flowers upon it in green."[14] The Queen was so delighted with the finished tea set and some other pieces that Wedgwood sent for her inspection, that she named him "Potter to Her Majesty." This appointment was probably confirmed in the summer of 1767.[15] Henceforth, Wedgwood called his cream-colored ware "Queen's Ware," and reaped the benefits of royal patronage.

Although Wedgwood was very pleased with the Queen's Ware and hoped that it would be a success, he still continued to make the more traditional types of ceramics. His business was rapidly expanding and America was a major market. On March 2, 1765, Josiah wrote to his friend and patron, Sir William Meredith:

> The bulk of our particular Manufactures you know are exported to foreign markets, for our home consumption is very trifling in comparison to what are sent abroad, and the principal of these markets are the Continent and Islands of N. America. To the Continent we send an amazing quantity of white stoneware and some of the finer kinds, [Agate, Cauliflower, etc.] but for the Islands we cannot make anything too rich and costly.[16]

Queen's Ware Husk *pattern plate with puce hand-painted decoration. Shards of this pattern have been found at excavations at Williamsburg, Virginia. ca. 1770. Diameter 9½ inches (24 cm.). Impressed Wedgwood.*

Juſt Opened, and to be Sold by

JOHN JENKINS,

Near the Elm Tree, and oppoſite John Foſter's, Eſq;
very cheap for Caſh,

A NEAT Aſſortment of QUEEN's WARE,
viz.

Cups and Saucers	Plates and Diſhes
Tea Pots	Muſtard Pots
Biſhops	Potting Pots
Bowls	Sauce Boats
Mugs and Jugs	Salts
Patty and Baking Pans	Chamber Pots, &c.

Alſo Spices of all Sorts, Loaf and brown Sugar,
Tea, Coffee and Chocolate, Raiſins, Rice, Indico,
Ginger, Copperas, Allum, Redwood, Brimſtone,
Needles, Pins, Threads, Fiſh Hooks, &c.

N. B. China Bowls and Glaſs Ware riveted with
Silver or Braſs, in the neateſt Manner.---Enquire of
LEWIS JENKINS.

Advertisement for Wedgwood's Queen's Ware from Providence Gazette, *March 16, 1771.*

Wedgwood was enjoying the first fruits of hard-won success, but he was worried about the future of his business, as the next few lines indicate.

> This trade to our Colonies we are apprehensive of loseing in a few years as they have set on foot some Potworks there already, and have at this time an agent amongst us hireing a number of our hands for establishing a new Pottsworks in South Carolina, haveing got one of our insolvent Master Potters there to conduct them, haveing material there equal if not superior to our own for carrying on that Manufactorie; and as the necessaries &c of life and consequently the price of Labour amongst us are daily upon the advance, I make no question but more will follow them and join their Brother artists and Manufacturers of every class, who are from all quarters takeing rapid flight indeed the same way! Whether this evil can be remedyed is out of our sphere to know, but we cannot help apprehending such consequences from these emigrations as make us very uneasy for our trade and our Posterity.[17]

Wedgwood probably need not have worried. The competition he feared from the colonies never materialized, and Queen's Ware enjoyed a tremendous vogue. One year later Wedgwood wrote that "the demand for this sd. *Creamcolour, Alias, Queen's Ware, Alias, Ivory,* still increases. It is really amazing how rapidly the use of it has spread almost over the whole Globe, & how universally it is liked."[18] With this great success in hand, Wedgwood was determined to break away from many of the traditional types of ceramics and continue promoting Queen's Ware.

> I am quite clearing my wareho. of colour'd ware [tortoise shell, agate, cauliflower, etc.], am heartily sick of the commodity and have been so long but durst not venture to quit it 'till I had something better in hand, which thanks to my fair customers I now intend to make the most of it.[19]

Most of the leftover colored ware was destined for North America. Josiah instructed his agent, John Wedgwood, to "sell the Green and Gold for Pensacola, the new discov'd Islands, or where you can, for I will never take it again, so make your best of it." Wedgwood added, "I am quite clearing my warehouse of Colord ware — Green desert ware is often wanted, in *reality* for the West India Islands — I have a few crates on hand, some gilt, some plain, Ergo-shod be glad to part with them on very moderate terms."[20]

By September 1767, most of the colored ware had been disposed of satisfactorily. "I am rejoyced to know you have shipd off the Green & Gold — May the winds & seas be propitious & the *invaluable* Cargo be wafted in safety to their destined Market for the emolument of our American brethren and friends."[21]

Besides being interested in America as a market for his wares, Wedgwood was also seriously interested in the colonies as a source of raw materials. In 1767 he commissioned Thomas Griffiths, who had briefly been a planter in South Carolina, to secure for him some Cherokee clay, which was reputed to be of very fine quality and very white in color; as he described it above in his letter to Meredith, "equal if not superior to our own." Griffiths kept a diary of his time in America as Wedgwood's agent. He had taken on a difficult and dangerous task and was plagued with bad weather, bad luck, and misunderstandings with the Cherokee Indians. By the time he finally got back to London with six tons of the clay, it had cost Wedgwood a total of about £500. Unfortunately, Wedgwood found that the Cherokee clay was not significantly superior to the clays available nearby. He did, however, continue to be interested in clay deposits in the New World and in one of his notebooks he recorded the existence of promising clay deposits in Florida, near Pensacola Bay, and at the Delaware River, one hundred miles north of Philadelphia. Today a commemorative sign stands in Franklin, South Carolina, near the spot where Griffiths obtained samples of the clay for Wedgwood.

Much of the ware Wedgwood shipped to America was transfer-printed (rather than hand-painted) Queen's Ware. Transfer printing was a decorative technique perfected by John Sadler and Guy Green of Liverpool in about 1755.[22] Briefly, the

Queen's Ware Beaded edge plate and Bunker mug decorated with black transfer printing and enriched with added color. The ships depicted on these pieces are often referred to as "Clipper" ships. The term is a misnomer, since the first true Clipper ship was not built until 1845. Plate: ca. 1785. Diameter 11¼ inches (28.5 cm.). Impressed Wedgwood, B, 7. Mug: ca. 1785. Height 6 inches (15 cm.). Impressed Wedgwood, 5, ( ).

technique involved engraving on copper plates in much the same way as was done for book illustrations, but a special ink and a very strong, thin tissue paper were used. The paper conformed to the shape of the ceramic piece when it was pressed on to transfer the ink impression. The printing was done on "biscuit," a piece that had already been fired once. After the printing, the piece was fired a second time in order to remove oils in the ink. Then it was glazed and fired a third and final time.

From 1761 to 1800 virtually all of Wedgwood's transfer-printed Queen's Ware was done by Sadler and Green. Wedgwood apparently experimented with printing on biscuit himself in 1784, but found the arrangement with Sadler and Green more to his satisfaction. Transfer-printed ceramics became a major item of production at the Wedgwood pottery. The technique was especially well suited to the production of commemorative ware, and indeed, much of Wedgwood's transfer-printed Queen's Ware was intended for display, rather than for actual daily use. Transfer printing could, however, be used very effectively on dinnerware; a beautiful example of this is the Morris Monteith. The simple, almost delicate, transfer-printed design subtly emphasizes the elegant shape and rich cream color of the monteith. This particular piece was part of a dinner service made for Robert Morris, the great financier of the Revolution, while he was "Agent of Marine" for the Continental Navy from 1781 until 1785, when the Navy was disbanded. The monteith is decorated on two sides and on the bottom of the interior with the Seal of the Board of Admiralty. The Seal consists of a shield on which is an anchor and pattern of alternating stripes. Above the shield is a ship in full sail and below a banner with the motto, "Sustentans et Sustentatum," meaning "Sustaining and Sustained." The monteith was intended to be fine enough to grace the table of a man reputed to be the richest in America, and to be part of an impressive service that Morris could use when entertaining the Marquis de Lafayette and other distinguished visitors.

Throughout the Wedgwood company's more than two hundred years of continuous production, the artistic reputation of the firm has, to a great degree, been based upon their fine ornamental work, predominently in Jasper and Black Basalt. It is important to remember, however, that it was the production of useful ware that formed the basis for the company's continuing financial success.

*This Queen's Ware monteith with black transfer-printed decoration was used for cooling wine glasses. ca. 1781-1785. 6 x 12 inches (15 x 30 cm.). Impressed Wedgwood. Collection: **Independence National Historical Park**, Philadelphia, Pennsylvania, gift of Mrs. Samuel B. Oster.*

ORNAMENTAL WARE: PORTRAIT MEDALLIONS, BUSTS AND STATUES OF IMPORTANT FIGURES OF THE REVOLUTIONARY WAR ERA

A S Bruce Tattersall, Curator of the Wedgwood Museum in Barlaston, England, notes in the introduction to *Wedgwood Portraits and the American Revolution*, "the concept of a portrait, born in classicism and nutured in the Renaissance, came fully into its own in the eighteenth century."[23] He explains further:

> The medieval world, with its emphasis upon the crowd rather than the individual and its neo-Aristotelian ideas of perfection, was most unsympathetic to the idea of a portrait as a realistic representation. It was only when individuals began to be again considered of importance, and when a larger number of the population came to feel that it was valuable to know precisely what somebody looked like, that portraiture could again flourish. Increasing education in Europe and Britain, combined with the invention of engraving, led to the popularisation of images of the great.[24]

In addition to engravings, cameos and medals were in great demand. Likenesses of famous individuals were done in ivory, precious metals, plaster, wax and any other materials that were suited to being carved or molded. With his development of Jasper in 1774, Josiah Wedgwood had the perfect material for making cameos and medallions quickly, in large quantities, and cheaply.

A list of the subjects of Wedgwood's portrait medallions reads like a veritable *Who's Who* of the eighteenth century. Scientists, writers, musicians, politicians, kings and queens can all be found on Wedgwood medallions and cameos. If the market demanded a particular face, Wedgwood produced it, and he rarely let his own personal opinions interfere with his business sense. Wedgwood produced likenesses of several American Revolutionary War heroes, but he also produced likenesses of the Englishmen who were so bitterly opposed to them. Portraits of Franklin sold well in France; that fact was of major importance to Wedgwood during the war when his wares could no longer reach the American market.

The person most frequently portrayed on Wedgwood portrait medallions and cameos was King George III. Historical assessment of the role that George III played in the course of the Revolutionary War has been revised again and again throughout the years. He has been variously described as a madman, a despot, a weak ruler totally dependent upon his advisors, and a cunning and ruthless individual whose policies were directly responsible for the Revolution. Most historians agree that George III was probably not a particularly talented, creative, or charismatic leader; however, despite his personal shortcomings and despite the fact that his bouts with madness meant that increasingly more power was assumed by Parliament, the King was very concerned about his place in history. After committing himself to a certain course of action toward America, he felt that any compromise would pave the way for uprisings in other British colonies. In 1779 he wrote:

> The present contest with America I cannot help seeing as the most serious in which any country was ever engaged. It contains such a train of consequences that they must be examined to feel its real weight. Whether the laying a tax was deserving all the evils that have arisen from it I suppose no man could allege without being thought fitter for Bedlam than a seat in the senate; but step by step the demands of America have risen. Independence is their object, which every man not willing to sacrifice every object to a momentary and inglorious peace must concur with me in thinking this country can never submit to. Should America succeed in that, the West Indies must follow, not in independence, but for their own interest they must become dependent of America. Ireland would soon follow and this island reduced to itself, would be a poor island indeed.[25]

Lavender and white Jasper Dip portrait medallion of King George modeled by William Hackwood from an original by Isaac Gossett (1713-1799), a prominent wax portraitist. ca. 1775-1776. 4 x 3 1/8 inches (10 x 8 cm.). Impressed Wedgwood, Geo 3^d, inscribed in gold George the Third.

Black Basalt portrait medallion of King George III from a wax portrait variously ascribed to Henry Burch Jnr. and Isaac Gosset. ca. 1780. 4 1/4 x 3 1/4 inches (10.5 x 7.8 cm.). Impressed Wedgwood C 11, 32.

Although Wedgwood undoubtedly did not agree with the King and his advisors, he did not let his own feelings determine the productions of the company. Likenesses of the King were in demand in England, and Wedgwood issued several versions, none of which portrayed the King as anything other than dignified, statesmanly, and beloved by his subjects.

One man, who like Wedgwood was an early advocate of American freedom, was in a somewhat better position to aid the American cause. William Pitt (1708-1778), who was later named first Earl of Chatham, was the first among English politicians in the House of Commons to propose and fight for a policy of understanding toward the colonies. Though he was considered by many of his peers to be an extremist, his position was in fact fairly conservative, and was designed to win broad support among the British people and to enhance his political future. Chatham viewed the American demands as a crucial test of the viability of the principles on which the British Constitution was based. Consequently, although he believed that the colonists should nôt be taxed without adequate representation in Parliament, and supported religious tolerance and freedom of the press, he felt that all of these conditions should be worked out within the political framework of the British Commonwealth and thus did not favor independence as a solution.

Portraits of Chatham were common. He was a popular subject and his portrait was painted by the American artists John Singleton Copley and Charles Willson Peale, as well as by several British artists. Likenesses of Chatham were also done by the sculptor Joseph Wilton and by Wedgwood. Often after an original, formal portrait was painted, it was copied by the original artist or others in oils or was produced in mezzotint or other inexpensive forms. Consequently, a single portrait could have enormous impact as it was reproduced in various media.

Around 1766 Wedgwood produced barrel-shaped Queen's Ware jugs decorated with black transfer-printed designs of a half-length portrait of Pitt. The engraving was done by Thomas Billinge after the painting by William Hoarde. Wedgwood wrote the following to Bentley in July, 1776, while Chatham was very popular in America.

> What do you think of sending Mr. Pitt on crockery ware to America; a quantity might certainly be sold there now, and some advantage made of the American prejudice in favor of that man. Lord Gower brought his family to see my works the other day and asked me if I had not sent Mr. Pitt over in shoals to America. If you happen to do anything in that way, we can divide a tolerable profit and sell at the same price with Sadler.[26]

Black Basalt bust of William Pitt, first Earl of Chatham, after a bust by Joseph Wilton, R.A. ca. 1775. Height 25 inches (63 cm.). Impressed Wedgwood & Bentley.

Chatham's popularity later ebbed somewhat when it became obvious that his espousal of the American cause did not extend to supporting independence. In fact, soon the Tories claimed him as *their* hero. John Singleton Copley, a Tory whose father-in-law had lost £15,000 worth of tea during the Boston Tea Party, painted an emotionally charged picture entitled *Death of the Earl of Chatham*. The scene is Chatham's last speech before the House of Lords in 1778, when he rose to defend the monarchy and the commonwealth and to denounce what he felt were violent and indefensible tactics on the part of the American revolutionaries and their allies. During the course of his argument Chatham collapsed, and he died a few weeks later.

In addition to the transfer-printed commemorative pieces, Wedgwood & Bentley also issued a large, dramatic bust of Chatham in Black Basalt. Chatham is depicted with a solemn and dignified expression and is shown draped in classical robes. This is one of the most sensitive and respectful portraits of Chatham, who was during his lifetime often the subject of vitriolic political cartoons accusing him of demagoguery and ambition.

Black Basalt portrait medallion of Charles James Fox attributed to John Flaxman after a 1784 portrait by Sir Joshua Reynolds. ca. 1790. 4 1/8 x 3 1/4 inches (10.5 x 8.5 cm.). Impressed Wedgwood.

Another of America's early supporters in Parliament was Charles James Fox (1749-1806). Fox was born to a family which had been active in public service for more than a century, and took his own seat in Parliament in November of 1768, at the age of nineteen. Charles's father, Lord Holland, doted upon his son and, according to all reports, allowed him an indulgent and unrestrained childhood. Fox grew up to be a man of considerable charm—all life, spirit, motion, and good humor. When he entered Parliament in 1768, he was well educated and articulate, but his political opinions were yet unformed. In a sense, Fox was a young man looking for a cause when he entered Parliament; he emerged as one of the staunchest supporters of the American right to independence.

In 1768 Parliament was a hotbed of factionalism, debate, and intrigue. It had become a political and social arena in which men fought desperately for the attention and support of the King. The situation of the American colonies became an issue closely allied with parliamentary authority and monarchal prerogative, and as such it became the target for heated debates only remotely associated with the real problems between England and the colonies. Fox, who for a short time had cultivated the image of an independent, soon used the American question to forge an alliance between himself and other members of Parliament who opposed the Crown's policy toward America and who were resentful of Chatham's influence with the King. He and Edmund Burke, among others, spoke out repeatedly against the war with America and pleaded for a negotiated settlement. Their courage should not be underestimated. Once the hostilities with America had escalated into open warfare, it became increasingly difficult for Fox and his associates to carry on anything resembling a "patriotic" opposition to the expressed policy of the King and his advisors. However, it is also important to restrain any tendency to glamorize Fox's conduct during the American Revolution. He constantly opposed the government, but his opposition was prompted as much by the exigencies of parliamentary politics as by any regard for principle.

Josiah Wedgwood was extremely interested in the course of the war between England and America, and he studied the current events closely. He may have had in mind many American heroes he would have liked to have portrayed on cameos and medallions, but there were certain constraints which prevented his issuing portraits of the Americans he admired. As "Potter to the Queen," Wedgwood was in a rather delicate position if he chose to produce portraits of the King's adversaries. Also, once trade between England and America had come to a halt, his market for American subjects was severely restricted. However, certain American heroes (especially those well known in France) were portrayed by Wedgwood during the war.

Benjamin Franklin was one American whose likeness was produced by Wedgwood on several occasions. Although he never met him personally, Wedgwood admired Benjamin Franklin greatly. Besides having mutual friends in the Lunar Society, the two men had certain characteristics in common. Both supported American independence, and both had liberal attitudes toward the rights of private individuals. Further, both had great interest in and respect for scientific methodology; Franklin's experiments with electricity are justifiably famous, and Josiah Wedgwood's careful experiments with ceramic materials and techniques, though less widely known, were considered sophisticated in his day. In fact, Wedgwood was elected a Fellow of the prestigious Royal Academy shortly after he published the results of his experimentation. In light of his professed admiration for Franklin, it is not surprising that Wedgwood produced several portrait medallions of that distinguished American.

One of the most widely reproduced portraits of Franklin was designed by the sculptor Jean Baptiste Nini (1717-1786).[27] This portrait was originally done in terra cotta, and was signed and dated, NINI/F 1777. On the *tranche* of the shoulder, Nini placed a coat of arms with a lightning rod and thunderbolt as an allusion to Franklin's role as a scientist. Nini was born in Urbino, Italy, but in 1772, he went to France to head the glass and pottery works of Jacques Donatien Le Ray de Chaumont. Le Ray

Left: *Terra cotta portrait medallion of Benjamin Franklin by Jean Baptiste Nini. 1777. Diameter 4 3/8 inches (11 cm). Signed and dated Nini F 1777. Right: Detail of medallion showing signature and coat of arms on* tranche *of the shoulder.*

was Franklin's host when the latter was in France between 1777 and 1785. Jean Gorely, writing in 1940, says that although Nini was short and grotesque (probably crippled) he "had excellent taste and much talent." Gorely adds, "Both Le Ray and Franklin honored him with their friendship. Franklin became the subject for at least nine of the sixty-four portrait medallions assigned to Nini. In 1777, Nini did five versions of the American, in 1778, two versions, and in 1779, two more, some with spectacles, some with the cap of liberty, and some bareheaded."[28]

Whether Franklin formally sat for these portraits is unknown. Louise Todd Ambler reports that on June 17, 1777 in a letter to Thomas Walpole, Franklin mentions that some terra cotta medallions had been produced. "From a Sketch . . . drawn by

Blue and white Jasper portrait medallion of Benjamin Franklin after Nini medallion of 1777. ca. 1951, from eighteenth-century mold. 4 1/2 x 3 1/4 inches (11.5 x 8.5 cm.). Impressed Wedgwood, J, Franklin.

Neoclassical portrait medallion of Benjamin Franklin by William Hackwood. Pale blue Jasper body with darker blue dip and white relief. This portrait is said to be adapted from a wax by Isaac Gosset or from one of Nini's many portraits of Franklin. ca. 1775-1777. 2 1/8 x 1 7/8 inches (5.5 x 4.6 cm.). Impressed Wedgwood & Bentley, Dr. Franklin.

A second version of William Hackwood's neoclassical portrait of Franklin in Black Basalt. The difference is most apparent in the treatment of the hair. ca. 1775-1777. 4 x 3 1/4 inches (10.2 x 8.3 cm.). Impressed Wedgwood & Bentley.

Blue and white Jasper portrait medallion of Benjamin Franklin after bust by Jean Jacques Caffiéri about 1777. Caffiéri had been able to arrange sittings with Franklin, and this stern portrait is probably a very good likeness. ca. 1968, from eighteenth-century mold. 2 3/4 x 2 inches (7 x 5.2 cm.). Impressed B. Franklin. Collection: Milton Aion.

your ingenious and valuable Son, they have made here Medallions in *terra cuit.* A Dozen have been presented to me, and I think he has a Right to one of them."[29] The Walpole drawing is now lost, so it is difficult to judge how much Nini was indebted to Walpole for his conception of Franklin's portrait. It is interesting to note the fur hat that Franklin wears in the Nini portrait. This is quite unlike the hat that Franklin normally wore, which is more accurately depicted in an engraving by Augustin de Saint Aubin after a drawing by Charles Nicholas Cochin. The cap that Franklin wears in the Nini medallion is derived from portraits of Jean Jacques Rosseau.[30] Whether intentionally or not, Nini thus provided a visual link between Franklin and the French *philosophes.*

Blue and white Jasper portrait medallion of Franklin (ca. 1775) wearing court dress and curled wig. Since Franklin never indulged in the latter fashion, it is understandable that this medallion was at one time thought to be a likeness of Josiah Wedgwood's friend, Dr. John Fothergill. Patience Wright, an American artist and alleged Revolutionary spy, and Isaac Gosset have each been proposed as the original modeler of this unusual portrait. ca. 1968, from eighteenth-century mold. 6 1/8 x 4 3/4 inches (15.5 x 12 cm.). Impressed Benjamin Franklin. Collection: Milton Aion.

Shortly after the Nini medallion was produced at Le Ray's pottery, Wedgwood produced a similar version in blue and white Jasper modeled by William Hackwood. This was not, however, the first portrait of Franklin issued by the English firm. A classical-style portrait of Franklin had been modeled by Hackwood around 1775, shortly after Wedgwood perfected his technique for making Jasper. This early date is evidence of Wedgwood's own high regard for the man, and of his belief that Franklin's popularity in Europe would create a strong demand for portraits. Several other portrait medallions of Franklin were made by Wedgwood, including a second version of the Hackwood neoclassical portrait, a portrait based on a bust by Jean Jacques Caffieri, and one very elaborate portrait after a contemporary wax likeness.

It is interesting to note that Wedgwood produced portraits of two other members of the Franklin family. A medallion of Benjamin Franklin's son, William Franklin (1731-1813), is listed in the company's 1787 sales catalogue. William was appointed Governor of New Jersey in 1763, but during the hostilities between England and America he favored the monarchy, and his arrest was ordered by the Provincial Congress of New Jersey. He was forced to flee to England in 1782. William's son, William Temple Franklin (1760-1823), was also the subject of a Wedgwood portrait medallion. The medallion is attributed to Flaxman around 1783, and appears in the 1788 catalogue. William Temple Franklin acted as secretary to his grandfather in Paris, and later edited an edition of his works.[31]

Blue and white Jasper Dip portrait of William Franklin attributed to John Flaxman. ca. 1784-1790.
4 1/8 x 3 1/4 inches (10.7 x 8.2 cm.). Impressed Wedgwood, G/ Franklin.

Portraits of George Washington have been produced in many forms by the Wedgwood company throughout its history. Medallions, busts, statues, and plates have all been issued in his honor. In the eighteenth century Wedgwood produced a blue and white Jasper medallion of Washington in the same nonclassical style as the Franklin medallion mentioned above. This particular portrait has been variously identified as Washington, Chatham, and Roscoe. At one point the Wedgwood firm issued medallions from this mold impressed "Chatham;" the design, however, was originally intended to be Washington. The portrait was adapted from a medal supposedly designed by Voltaire and struck in France in 1777 or 1778.[32] Wedgwood published his version of the portrait a year or two later.

Neoclassical portrait medallion of George Washington after a medal said to have been designed by Voltaire. Blue Jasper body with darker blue dip and white relief. ca. 1778-1779. 2 x 1 7/8 inches (5.4 x 4.6 cm.). Impressed Wedgwood & Bentley.

In the 1900s, Wedgwood produced a Black Basalt bust of Washington after an original eighteenth-century bust by Jean-Antoine Houdon (1741-1828). Houdon had been urged by Franklin and Jefferson to come to America to sculpt a likeness of Washington from life, before the chance to do so was lost forever. On June 22, 1784, the Virginia State Assembly, prodded by Jefferson, passed a resolution "to take measures for procuring a statue of General Washington to be of the finest marble, and best workmanship . . . "[33] Houdon accepted the commission and traveled to Mount Vernon in 1785, where he made a life mask, several terra cotta busts, and a great many sketches of Washington in preparation for the statue, which was completed in France.

Black Basalt bust of George Washington after eighteenth-century bust by Jean Antoine Houdon. ca. 1876. Height 13 inches including plinth (33 cm.). Impressed Wedgwood.

25

In addition to the statue, Houdon also sculpted several busts of Washington. His work was an immediate success and was widely copied and adapted for reproduction in various media. Plaster casts of Houdon's Washington were installed in suitable rooms in gracious homes. Part of the reason for the popularity of Houdon's portrait is that Houdon did not produce a conventionally heroic and military figure, but rather captured Washington in a thoughtful and intimate pose; he endowed his subject with an individuality of expression that was unusual in late eighteenth-century sculpture.

Josiah Wedgwood apparently never chose Thomas Jefferson as the subject for a portrait medallion or bust; however, it would appear that there is some basis for linking their names historically. Not only was Jefferson instrumental in commissioning Houdon's *Washington* (later copied in Black Basalt by Wedgwood), but he also is said to have purchased several Wedgwood Jasper plaques that were used to decorate at least one of the chimney-pieces at Monticello. Alison Kelly mentions that Jefferson is known to have visited London in 1786, and suggests that he may have chosen the plaques himself. Kelly gives the following description of the chimney-piece at Monticello:

> The chimney-piece, like others in the house, has a rather deeper entablature than would have been found on an English piece of the same date, and to fit it as a centrepiece Jefferson chose a tablet of a squarer shape than was usually bought in England. He had one with only four *Muses* on it, instead of the usual five. This, however, need not have been a special order; one of this type was included in the 1781 sale, presumably from stock. On each side of this *Muses* panel, Jefferson had a bas-relief design of an urn, and, at the outer ends of the chimney-piece, Wedgwood plaques showing *Apollo* and *Urania*.[34]

The Wedgwood company has produced portraits of Jefferson in the twentieth century.

SLAVE MEDALLION

THE Slave Medallion was originally produced by Wedgwood in 1787 in black and white Jasper. Wedgwood, one of the ardent founders of The Society for the Suppression of the Slave Trade, directed his chief modeler, William Hackwood, to model the design for production as a cameo. Producing it in this form was a stroke of genius on Wedgwood's part. Cameos were then enjoying a vogue and the Wedgwood factory in Staffordshire had made a great many imitation cameos in Jasper. Most of these were charmingly romaticized versions of classical subjects in white on pastel backgrounds. Imagine the stir that the first Slave Medallions must have created. A strongly modeled Negro, kneeling, with his hands and feet bound in chains, appealed for freedom with the question, "Am I Not a Man and a Brother?"

Slave Medallion. 1787. 1 1/8 x 1 1/16 inches (3.0 x 2.7 cm.). Unmarked.

Wedgwood had thousands of these medallions made and distributed them free to anyone concerned with the abolition of slavery. In 1788 he sent some of the medallions to Benjamin Franklin in Philadelphia with the following letter:

> I embrace the opportunity of a packet making up by my friend W. Phillips to inclose for the use of Your Excellency and friends, a few Cameos on a subject which I am happy to acquaint you is daily more and more taking possession of men's minds on this side of the Atlantic as well as with you. It gives me great pleasure to be embarked on this occasion in the same great and good cause with you, Sir, and I ardently hope for the final completion of our wishes.

This will be an epoch before unknown to the world, and while relief is given to so many of our fellow creatures immediately the object of it, the subject of freedom itself will be more canvassed and better understood in the enlightened nations.

I labor at this moment under a rheumatic headache which has afflicted me some months, and this obliged me to use the hand of my nephew and prevents me also from saying more at present then begging, Sir, to be considered among the number of those who have the highest veneration for your virtues and gratitude for the benefits you have bestowed on Society.[35]

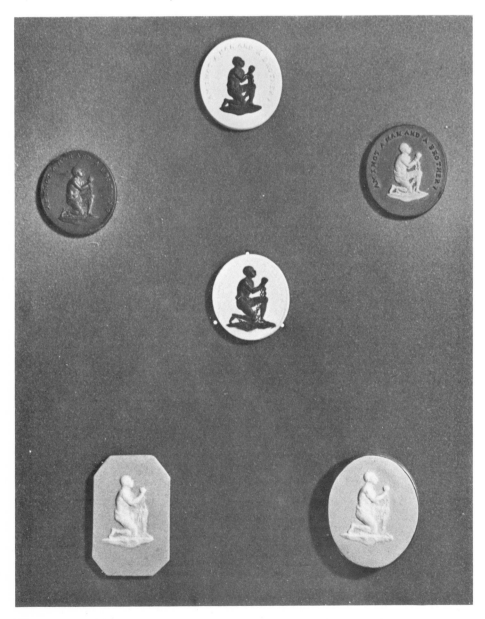

Other versions of the Slave Medallion; the one at top is an exact replica made especially for the Buten Museum of Wedgwood in 1976 to mark the American Bicentennial. Impressed Wedgwood Made in England, C 76, BMW.

Some months later, Franklin responded.

> I received the letter you did me the honour of writing to me the 29th of Feb. past, with your valuable Pieces of Cameos, which I am distributing among my Friends, and in whose countenances I have seen such Mark of being affected by contemplating the Figure of the Suppliant (which is admirably executed) that I am persuaded it may have a Effect equal to that of the best written Pamphlet, in procuring favour to those oppressed People. Please accept my hearty Thanks, and believe me to be, with great esteam.

Sir, your most obedient servant
B. Franklin[36]

Franklin's prediction concerning the impact of the medallions was probably accurate. It became quite the fashion to wear them set in hatpins, bracelets, rings and belts. The Reverend Thomas Clarkson, one of the most active abolitionists, wrote that "the taste for wearing them became general, and thus fashion . . . was seen for once in the honourable office of promoting the cause of justice, humanity, and freedom."[37] Franklin died in 1790. His last public act, as President of the Pennsylvania Society for promoting the Abolition of Slavery, was to sign an anti-slavery petition directed to Congress.[38]

Since it was first manufactured in 1787, the Slave Medallion has been reissued in many different color combinations and in various shapes and sizes. The medallion is important both for the artistic merit of the design and for the historical significance of its message and purpose.

WEDGWOOD AND THE UNITED STATES AFTER 1783

Despite increased competition, Wedgwood was successful in regaining a sizeable portion of the ceramics market in America after the end of the Revolutionary War in 1783, but by 1790 Josiah had given up an active role in the company, and had turned the business over to his sons and nephew, Thomas Byerley (1747-1810). Wedgwood's sons were not very enthusiastic about the business; Thomas dropped out of the firm because of chronic ill health, John entered the banking profession, and Josiah II settled in Surrey as a gentleman farmer. Byerley, who had worked for Wedgwood since 1775, was growing old and, in any case, had never shown conspicuous talent for business management. When Josiah died in 1795, the company was left essentially leaderless. In addition, there were serious problems that were affecting the entire pottery industry. The French Revolution and, later, the Napoleonic Wars threw economic conditions in England and on the Continent into a turmoil. In addition to losing its markets abroad, the company was having difficulty continuing production at home. Costs were high; their skilled, experienced workers were joining the military; the quality of the products was slipping; and the company was losing money on its ornamental wares. Competitors were producing passable to good imitations of Wedgwood ceramics, and the neoclassical style that Josiah has pioneered was becomming passé. A great deal of high-quality, inexpensive porcelain was being imported from China and was extremely popular. Thus, the closing years of the eighteenth century and the beginning of the nineteenth mark a period of relatively unstable profits for the Wedgwood company. As Ralph M. Hower points out, "in such circumstances even the most aggressive management would have found it difficult to carry the Wedgwood business much beyond the point where the first Josiah had left it."[39] Due to the paucity of business records for the period up to 1895, it is difficult to trace the commercial activity of the Wedgwood company for most of the nineteenth century. It is obvious, however, that the company was aware that it would have to initiate new products and new marketing strategies in order to maintain its position in the rapidly changing marketplace. In 1802, Byerley suggested that the company produce "something like the old French Fayance," because their usual earthenware was "becoming so common that it will very soon grow out of fashion."[40] In 1807 he complained that business had still not increased and said that "though the town is very full, our [London showrooms] are very empty most days."[41]

The early nineteenth century was a period of great experimentation by the company. Under the leadership of Josiah Wedgwood II, who replaced Byerley in 1804, Wedgwood introduced six new types of ceramics: bas-relief ware, drab ware, lustre (Moonlight, Steel, Platinum), celadon, blue-printed ware, and Egyptian hieroglyphic relief ware. New sales techniques were also considered. However, despite all this activity, the partners repeatedly complained about slim profits. Hower suggests that this may be explained by the fact that although the company registered large profits on paper, Wedgwood apparently was having difficulty collecting on some accounts.[42] America continued to be an important, but unstable, market for Wedgwood wares; business seesawed between prosperity and recession. By the end of the nineteenth century conditions were very bleak, and Wedgwood welcomed the commission to produce the Roosevelt White House China in 1902. They hoped that the ensuing publicity would spur sales in the United States.

In the nineteenth century busts and statues were popular; interest in portraiture continued to be strong. Commemorative and souvenir items sold well. Special pieces were issued to mark important events, and novelty items were produced to be sold at concessions at fairs and parks, and by social-service groups.

A very interesting and especially fine nineteenth-century Wedgwood portrait is the Parian bust of Abraham Lincoln issued shortly after his death in 1865. The craggy profile, sunken eyes, and touseled hair make this an especially sensitive and affecting portrait of the war-weary President. Lincoln is shown wearing a classical toga characteristic of Wedgwood busts. A few Black Basalt copies of this bust exist, including the one owned by the Buten Museum.

Modern Black Basalt version of Wedgwood's nineteenth-century Parian bust of Abraham Lincoln. ca. 1930. Height 17 inches (42.6 cm.). Impressed Wedgwood sans serif on plinth, Wedgwood Made in England on body.

Busts, such as the one of Lincoln, were large and expensive. Only the rich could purchase them and place them in properly dignified and important settings. For people of modest means, Wedgwood produced smaller pieces of statuary and also jugs and plates decorated with printed or relief portraits. An eight-inch Bone China statue of

George Washington (illustrated on the front cover) and a slightly larger Basalt allegorical statue entitled "America" are examples that date from the latter part of the nineteenth century. Charles L. Eastlake, arbiter of "Good Taste" in both England and America during the mid-1800s, records how statues such as these were used in interior decoration.

> It used to be the fashion to place a plaster urn or bust at the top of each bookcase, to give what upholsterers call a "finish" to the room. Urns are, however, but meaningless things in these days of Christian burial; and busts at so high an elevation, especially in a small room, convey a very distorted notion of the features which they represent. Large china bowls and vases may, however, be seen to advantage in such a place, and failing them, statuettes may be recommended.[43]
>
> * * * * *
>
> It is . . . by no means necessary to good effect that . . . drawings or paintings thus arranged should come into close contact. On the contrary, it is often a much better plan to separate them, especially in a drawing-room, by such small objects as sconces, small ornamental mirrors, or little wooden brackets supporting statuettes, vases, &c.[44]

Black Basalt allegorical statue of "America." ca. 1880. Height 14 inches (34.6 cm.). Impressed Wedgwood. Collection: Mrs. Seal Simons-Newmark.

Illustration from Charles L. Eastlake's Hints on Household Taste *(1878 ed.) showing preferred setting for ornamental bust.*

Another way to add variety to what Eastlake referred to as "wall-furniture," was by purchasing medallions, such as the one Wedgwood produced of Oliver Wendell Holmes. The medallion of Holmes was produced in 1895, one year after the poet's death, and was probably intended primarily for the American market. Holmes, now remembered chiefly for his poems "Old Ironsides" and "The Chambered Nautilus," was born in 1809 to a wealthy Boston family. After receiving his medical degree from Harvard, he pursued a career in medicine as professor of anatomy at Dartmouth. He published two important medical books, *Homeopathy and Its Kindred Delusions* (1842) and *The Contagiousness of Puerperal Fever* (1843). In addition to his medical career, Holmes was also active in the literary world. He was an urbane and witty conversationalist, a sought-after lecturer, and a militant Unitarian. He was also a leading contributor to the *Atlantic Monthly* and the author of many significant essays and poems. The medallion of Holmes issued by Wedgwood is a serious and sensitive portrait of this many-faceted man. Holmes appears to be absorbed in thought, brows knitted, hair rumpled. The medallion is dark blue Jasper Dip with white relief.

Dark blue Jasper Dip portrait medallion of Oliver Wendell Holmes. 1895. 6 1/2 x 4 3/4 inches (16.6 x 12 cm.). Impressed Wedgwood, O. W. Holmes.

As mentioned earlier, in the nineteenth century commemorative and souvenir items were very popular. In the Buten Museum collection there are six jugs of the period which are typical of this type of ware. Two of the jugs were produced to commemorate the Centennial celebration of American independence. The cane-colored Queen's Ware jug is decorated with dark brown prints of Independence Hall in 1776 and Memorial Hall in 1876. In relief on the molded band are the names of the thirteen original colonies; the dates 1776 and 1876 are in relief on the handle. The Majolica jug is decorated with relief portraits of George Washington and Abraham Lincoln and glazed in characteristic Majolica colors—blue, green, brown and red. These jugs were probably sold at concession booths right at the fairgrounds. The Centennial jugs demonstrate how ceramic pieces can be useful as historical documents. In addition to recording the contemporary appearances of buildings, places and events, they also record what was important to people at the time; for example, the Majolica Centennial jug shows that in the decade following his death, Lincoln took his place beside Washington as one of the greatest of American Presidents.

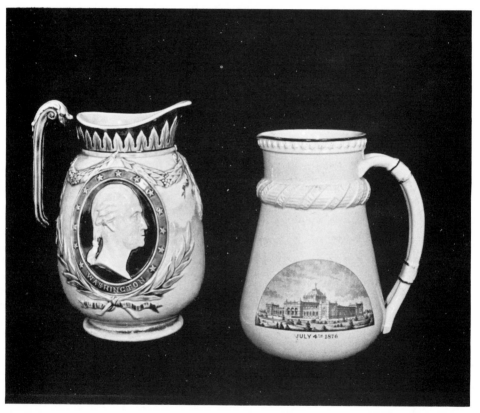

Pair of commemorative jugs celebrating the American Centennial in 1876. Left: Majolica jug. 1875. Height 8 inches (22 cm.). Impressed Wedgwood, Registry Mark, CQD, 6, W. Right: Cane-colored Queen's Ware jug. ca. 1876. Height 7 1/2 inches (19 cm.). Impressed Wedgwood, three letter mark.

Locally important events were also marked with special ceramics. The Rhode Island Jug in green and white Jasper commemorates the founding of the city of Providence by Roger Williams in 1636 and Rhode Island's admission to statehood in 1790. The Roger Williams Jug, produced by Wedgwood in 1886, commemorates the 200th anniversary of the founding of Providence. It is Queen's Ware with rich brown decorative printing.

Pair of jugs commemorating Rhode Island history. Left: Queen's Ware jug with brown transfer printing. ca. 1886. Height 4 3/4 inches (12 cm.). Imprinted Roger Williams Jug Made By J. Wedgwood & Son's Etruria for Messrs Warren & Wood Providence Rhode Island. Right: Green Jasper Dip jug. ca. 1895. Height 5 3/4 inches, (14.7 cm.). Impressed Wedgwood, England, V, 24. Collection: Mr. and Mrs. S. Arthur Levy.

Other nineteenth century commemorative ceramics in the Buten Museum collection include the Garfield and Longfellow Jugs. James Abram Garfield became the twentieth President of the United States in 1881; however, shortly after the election he was shot by an assassin and died in September of 1881. The Garfield Jug is creamware decorated with a brown transfer-printed portrait of Garfield on one side and a pastiche of American symbols (flag, eagle, et cetera) on the other. The jug is handsomely

Queen's Ware jug produced for Inauguration of James Garfield. ca. 1880. Height 7 1/2 inches (19 cm.). Impressed Wedgwood, imprinted H 1015, Garfield Jug Made By J. Wedgwood & Son's Etruria.

decorated in rich colors—red, blue, green, brown and orange. Although the jug has Garfield's birthdate and the date of his Inauguration on it, the date of his death is not listed; therefore, one may assume that the jug was most likely produced in anticipation of Garfield's Inauguration in 1881 and not to commemorate his death. It is a rare piece.

Detail of jug showing transfer-printed portrait of Henry Wadsworth Longfellow. 1880. Height 6 1/2 inches (16.5 cm.). Impressed Wedgwood, three letter mark, imprinted Manufactured by Josiah Wedgwood & Sons Etruria for Richard Briggs Boston Register[d] in Great Britain and France Also in the United States.

Reverse of Longfellow Jug showing inscription from "Keramos." The jug is brilliantly decorated in shades of red, orange, brown and green, and touches of gilding.

The Longfellow Jug produced by Wedgwood in 1880 was commissioned by Richard Briggs, a Boston china merchant who admired the New England poet. The black and white transfer print that decorated one side of the jug was engraved from a photograph of Longfellow taken when he was seventy-two years old. The use of photographs as a design source for transfer printing became common in the late nineteenth century. Earlier, paintings, etchings and mezzotints had served as sources. The use of photography opened new possibilities for portraits and decorative scenes. Briggs sent the photograph of Longfellow to Wedgwood along with the first seven lines of the poem "Keramos," which were printed on the other side of the jug.

> Turn, turn, my wheel! Turn round and round
> Without a pause, without a sound;
> So spins the flying world away!
> This clay, well mixed with marl and sand,
> Follows the motion of my hand;
> For some must follow and some command
> Though all are made of clay.

Five thousand of the jugs were made and sold for five dollars each. They were marketed in England and France as well as in the United States. Briggs presented one of the jugs to Longfellow as a New Year's gift in 1881.

During the late nineteenth century and well into the twentieth, Wedgwood commemorative ceramics were imported and marketed in the United States by the Boston firm of Jones, McDuffee & Stratton. Perhaps the most interesting ceramics handled by the firm were calendar tiles. These were made by Wedgwood from 1879 until 1926 expressly for the firm. The tiles had the calendar for the year printed on one side and a historical scene from in or around Boston on the other. Trinity Church; the Adam houses in Quincy, Massachusetts; and the Jones, McDuffee & Stratton Building on Franklin Street, Boston; can all be found pictured on calendar tiles. The tiles were distributed annually to customers of Jones, McDuffee & Stratton as souvenirs. Usually the printing was done in one color only, but some polychrome tiles were also made.

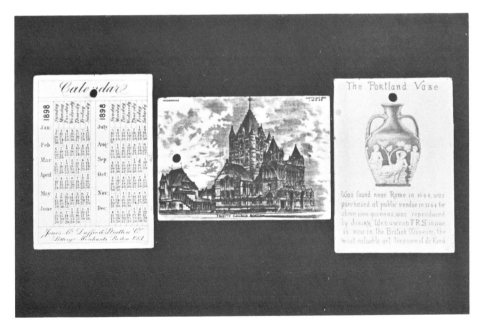

A selection of calendar tiles made for Jones, McDuffee & Stratton. ca. 1879-1929. 4 3/4 x 3 1/4 inches (12 x 8.3 cm.). Sometimes imprinted Wedgwood Etruria England.

In 1889 the Wedgwood company began manufacturing a series of plates known as "Old Historic Blue." The plates were advertised by Jones, McDuffee & Stratton as having historical scenes of places and events of interest to all Americans. Although the series was reminiscent of the Staffordshire Blue that was produced in the early years of the nineteenth century, the Wedgwood company did not copy any of the old scenes or border patterns. The Old Historic Blue plates were decorated with new transfer-printed engravings of historical areas in New York, Philadelphia, and New England. The plates were frequently used as wall decorations; a wooden molding or "plate rail" was fastened to the wall and the plates placed on it. Alternatively, the plates were set on the narrow shelves of a sideboard or "Welsh dresser."

The business relationship between Wedgwood and Jones, McDuffee & Stratton lasted about seventy-five years. In the 1950s, the Boston firm ceased to be an importer of commemorative ware, but the Wedgwood company continued to be a major manufacturer of this specialized type of ceramics.

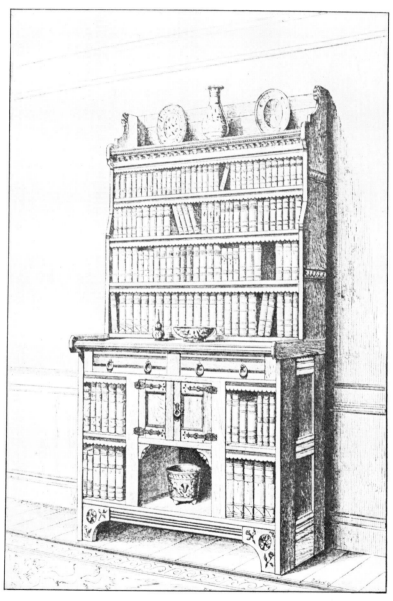

Illustration from Charles L. Eastlake's Hints on Household Taste *(1878 ed.) showing a library bookcase decorated with plates and other pottery.*

Selection of patriotic commemorative plates. Left: *"The Spirit of '76: Yankee Doodle."* 1904. *Diameter 9 1/4 inches (23.5 cm.). Impressed Wedgwood, L, three letter mark, imprinted Wedgwood Etruria England. Made for Daniel Low and Co., Salem, Massachusetts. Collection: Mr. and Mrs. S. Arthur Levy.* Center: *"National Capitol, Washington."* 1882. *Diameter 8 1/4 inches (21 cm.). Impressed Wedgwood GFK. Transfer-printed decoration in sepia.* Right: *Old Historic Blue commemorative plate, "The Capitol."* ca. 1900. *Diameter 9 1/8 inches (23.2 cm.). Impressed Wedgwood, three letter mark, imprinted Wedgwood Etruria England, Jones, McDuffee & Stratton trademark, Copyright 1900 J McD & S, The Capitol.*

THE TWENTIETH CENTURY

THE twentieth century began on an optimistic note for the Wedgwood company with their acceptance of an extraordinarily large and prestigious commission—the production of White House china for President Theodore Roosevelt. Shortly after beginning her duties as First Lady, Mrs. Roosevelt found that none of the china that had been used by previous administrations was sufficient for the social gatherings that she and the President planned to have at the White House. Mrs. Roosevelt requested assistance from the Van Heusen Charles Company of Albany, New York, importers of china, glass, and house furnishings, and Mr. Van Heusen took on the task of submitting a collection of china samples to the White House for inspection. Mrs. Roosevelt wanted a design which would be different and dignified, something which would be unmistakably known as "White House China." She also preferred to have the china made in the United States.[45]

With the help of leading artists and connoisseurs, the Roosevelts examined samples of seventy-eight designs which Van Heusen obtained for them. According to Margaret Brown Klapthor in *Official White House China*, an invaluable source of information about the Roosevelt service, the Roosevelts attempted to have the design they chose produced by an American pottery, but were not able to find a company that would accept the commission. An article entitled "Didn't Want Roosevelt Order" in *The Clay Record* of October 30, 1902, reported that the President had asked an American firm to make the china.

> An order from President Roosevelt for a $50,000 china set for the White House has been received by the Knowles, Taylor & Knowles Pottery Company, East Liverpool [Ohio]. After due deliberation the order was declined.
>
> It involved special shapes, a distinct line of decorations, and was a large order, involving so much interruption of regular business, or the erection of an entirely separate small plant for its production that its acceptance here was impracticable. The contract will probably be let to the celebrated Wedgwoods of England.
>
> That the company turned down the offer is regarded as remarkable.[46]

The Wedgwood company was, indeed, chosen to produce the design that the Roosevelts had selected. A transluscent cream-white Bone China body was decorated with a wide border of gold lines, which formed a lace-like pattern. The Great Seal of the United States was applied in color. It is interesting to note that the head of the eagle is turned toward the olive branch, indicating that the country was at peace.

The shapes of the pieces were designed by John E. Goodwin, Art Director of Wedgwood, and the decoration by Herbert Cholerton, decorator, artist, gilder and heraldic painter for the company. The dinner service was copyrighted and patented for exclusive use in the White House. A similar pattern, but without the Great Seal, is

Bread and butter plate from the Roosevelt White House dinner service. 1902. Diameter 6 inches (15.2 cm.). Imprinted Portland Vase Trademark, Wedgwood Made in England. Detail showing Great Seal of the United States.

called *Gold Colonnade,* and is still being produced by Wedgwood; however, the patent would preclude having any of the Roosevelt service reproduced for general sale to the public, as had happened in the case of White House services of previous Presidential administrations.

Another twentieth-century specially designed and commissioned ceramic pattern was Liberty China. During World War I, Mrs. Robert Coleman Taylor conceived the idea of producing china to raise money for war victims. She explained her idea in her book, *Liberty China and Queen's Ware.*

> When our country entered the Great War, I decided to have this chapter in our history commemorated by a patriotic china, to be made by a great potter and that I would devote all profits to the war sufferers.[47]

The china was designed by Mrs. Taylor herself. An American shield, circled by a wreath of laurel, was shown in the midst of the Allied flags. The emblem was purposely kept small and used as a coat of arms on the china. The only other decoration was a narrow band of gold around the edges of the pieces. The design was produced in both Queen's Ware and Bone China.

41

The china was manufactured by the Wedgwood company and imported and delivered by William A. Plummer & Company of New York. Liberty China was never advertised or publicly marketed. It was considered a special order and was shown only in Mrs. Taylor's drawing room; however, despite its limited promotion, the demand for the china far exceeded the supply. A total of 9,251 pieces were sold, raising $14,203.14 for war charities. In *Liberty China and Queen's Ware*, Mrs. Taylor listed the names of the subscribers, including President and Mrs. Wilson, Mrs. John D. Rockefeller, General Pershing, and other notables. One of Mrs. Taylor's stipulations in her contract with Wedgwood was that the orders for Liberty China would cease with the war's end and the copper plates for the design would be destroyed. This was done.

Examples of "Liberty China" shown with Mrs. Robert Coleman Taylor's book, Liberty China and Queen's Ware *(1000 copies privately printed by Doubleday, Page & Company, 1924). These are Queen's Ware pieces. ca. 1917. Teapot: Height 5 1/2 inches (13.8 cm.). Impressed Wedgwood England, three letter mark. Cup: Height 2 1/4 inches (5.5 cm.). Imprinted Wedgwood Etruria England. Saucer: 5 3/4 inches (14.5 cm.). Impressed Wedgwood, 3GT, imprinted Wedgwood Etruria England.*

An interesting type of post-World War I commemorative ware made by the Wedgwood company is "arms ware" made to commemorate American landmarks and cities. A small Black Basalt bud vase of this type is in the Buten Museum of Wedgwood collection. It is rather crudely decorated with the "civic crest" or city seal of Philadelphia in enamel colors. The seal is predominantly blue, yellow and orange, with touches of red, white and green. It is presumed that pieces such as this were sold as souvenirs; however, little is known about how these pieces were actually commissioned and marketed. Arms ware was also made to commemorate European and Canadian cities and landmarks. Judging from the pieces that survive, this ware was even more popular in Canada than in the United States.

Arms ware bud vase commemorating the city of Philadelphia. ca. 1930s. Height 5 inches (12.6 cm.). Impressed Wedgwood England.

*College plates. **Left:** plate commemorating Wheaton College, Wheaton, Illinois. Decorated in blue and yellow. ca. 1930s. Diameter 10 3/8 inches (26.3 cm.). Impressed Wedgwood, Made in England, imprinted Wedgwood Etruria England, Jones, McDuffee & Stratton trademark, inscription about the college's history. **Center:** plate made for the College of the City of New York. Transfer-printed decoration in puce. ca. 1940s. Diameter 10 3/4 inches (27.5 cm.). Impressed Wedgwood, imprinted Wedgwood of Etruria & Barlaston Made in England, The College of the City of New York, Townsend Harris Hall, Jones Mc-Duffee & Stratton trademark, portrait of Townsend Harris and autograph facsimile. **Right:** sample plate made for Bennett College, Greensboro, North Carolina. Coupe plate, 4709 shape, decoration in Williamsburg sepia from a drawing by Clare Leighton. 1952. Diameter, 10 1/2 inches (26.8 cm.). Impressed Wedgwood, imprinted Wedgwood of Etruria & Barlaston. Made in England, sample.*

In the 1930s, the firm of Jones, McDuffee & Stratton (for whom Wedgwood had made calendar tiles) began marketing plates decorated with views of school and college campuses. This type of commemorative ware, which was made especially for sale by colleges, schools, and other educational institutions, became the major area of business for the Boston company. Wedgwood produced the plates as a series for each client. Harvard University, for example, has had four series produced, totalling forty-eight views of the campus.

College commemorative ware is still produced by the Wedgwood company. It may be commissioned by a school organization, fund-raising group, alumni association, or other sponsor. Frequently Wedgwood reproduces sketches of the campus drawn by a famous graduate of the school or resident artist. In the past, college plates for Princeton University, Massachusetts Institute of Technology, and the University of Pennsylvania have been decorated with prints by artists affiliated with the universities. Occasionally the artist involved may be of national stature. Clare Leighton, known primarily for her very fine woodcuts, did drawings of Bennett College and Taft School. In addition to the college plates, Leighton also did a special series of twelve drawings for Wedgwood entitled "New England Industries." The designs included scenes of grist milling, farming, whaling, and logging.

Twentieth-century Wedgwood ware is particularly significant in terms of the amount of Jasper that was produced decorated with nonclassical subjects. John H. Thomas discussed the technique for making Jasper, as well as the company's increased use of nonclassical motifs, in a paper presented at the 1970 Wedgwood International Seminar. The first step in the production of Jasper is the making of an original clay model, which is several times larger than the required finished size. During successive firings at 1100° C., the model contracts to the desired size; the degree of contraction is usually about twenty percent. In order to maintain the precise detail the model is retouched after each firing. When a satisfactory model has been produced, molds

Original plaster model for portrait of John F. Kennedy. 1962. 14 x 12 inches (35 x 30 cm.). This massive plaster portrait is more than 1 1/2 inches in thickness. Impressed Jos. Wedgwood Barlaston, President Kennedy by Eric Owen 1962. Blue and white Jasper sweet dish with portrait of JFK ca. 1962. Diameter 4 3/8 inches (11 cm.). Impressed Wedgwood Made in England.

44

are cast from it. Reliefs are then made by filling the molds with soft clay, and then extracting the molded ornament by means of gentle suction. The relief is applied to the plain clay piece and fired.

With the exception of the final lapidary polish, which is now done by sand blasting, the technique is the same as that used by Josiah Wedgwood when he first perfected Jasper in 1776. In the twentieth century, especially since the 1950s, this body and technique, originally developed in order to imitate classical gems, have been used for more contemporary subjects. With very few exceptions, modern non-classical designs are the work of full-time modelers at Etruria and Barlaston, although the company occasionally uses the services of a free-lance artist. The chief modelers of nonclassical designs during this century have been Arnold Austin, his son Roy, and Eric Owen. Other important designers include Tom Harper (who designed *The Capitol* for the Charles Schwartz company, and also *Trinity Church at Newport, Rhode Island)*, Jesse Wilbraham, Peter Wall, Anna Zinkeisen, Arnold Machin and Richard Guyatt.

An interesting example of nonclassical Wedgwood ware is the blue and white Jasper ashtray made to commemorate Stanley Kubrick's movie *2001: A Space Odyssey*. Relief designs of the moon and a "Saturn" spaceship decorate the center; the border features the Lunar Excursion Module (or LEM) printed in gold.

Portraiture has remained a significant part of Wedgwood's total production. In this century portraits of American Presidents have been produced by Wedgwood in a variety of bodies. Franklin D. Roosevelt was a particularly popular subject. In 1945 Wedgwood produced a lavender Queen's Ware mug decorated with a cream-colored relief portrait of FDR. The mug, which was designed by Keith Murray and modeled by Arnold Machin, was one of a pair; its companion was a mug featuring a portrait

Queen's Ware bust of Franklin Delano Roosevelt. ca. 1940s. Height 7 1/2 inches (19 cm.). Impressed 5H43, imprinted Wedgwood of Etruria & Barlaston Made in England. Sample Queen's Ware Edme-shape plate decorated with transfer-printed portraits of Franklin and Eleanor Roosevelt. ca. 1960. Diameter 10 3/8 inches (26.3 cm.). Impressed Wedgwood 3 x 60, imprinted Wedgwood of Etruria & Barlaston Made in England, Engraved by the Wedgwood Studios, Designed Especially for Hyde Park Gift Shop, Hyde Park, New York, Sample.

of Winston Churchill. In addition to the mug, Wedgwood also issued a bust of Roosevelt and an Edme-shape commemorative plate with transfer-printed portraits of Franklin and Eleanor. Other presidents who have been portrayed by Wedgwood include Dwight D. Eisenhower, Harry Truman, John F. Kennedy, and Richard Nixon.

The celebration of the American Bicentennial in 1976 was the inspiration for a number of new commemorative designs. Wedgwood began designing and producing Bicentennial items as early as 1971. In December of that year Wedgwood announced the State Seal Series of compotiers in blue and white Jasper. A year later Wedgwood issued the first in a series of six Jasper plates commemorating events of the Revolutionary War. The series, designed by Tom Harper, included *The Boston Tea Party, Paul Revere's Ride, The Battle of Concord, Crossing the Delaware, Victory at Yorktown,* and *Signing of the Declaration of Independence.* In 1975, two more Bicentennial pieces were introduced: a handsome diced goblet in blue, white and sage green Jasper decorated with a portrait of Thomas Jefferson, and an impressive five-color Jasper Trophy plate in blue, white, cane, lilac and sage green decorated with a portrait of George Washington.

By April 1976, Wedgwood had introduced the full complement of Bicentennial items, including a new edition of the George Washington bust after Houdon that the company had first issued in the nineteenth century. In Jasper, there were two more Bicentennial items produced: the *Independence Plate* decorated with a central bas-relief of Independence Hall, Philadelphia, and the *Bicentennial Plates,* a pair of plates in blue and white, one featuring the state seals of the thirteen original colonies, and the other the signers of the Declaration of Independence. Two commemorative mugs completed the Wedgwood Bicentennial Collection: a two-handled Black Basalt "loving cup" with a gold American eagle design, and a Queen's Ware mug with a multicolored design of the American eagle and flag by Richard Guyatt.

In addition to the items comprising the Wedgwood Bicentennial Collection, the company also produced several commemorative designs that were specially commissioned for the Bicentennial. Among these were a set of thirteen Queen's Ware plates decorated with black transfer-printed decorations depicting scenes from the Revolutionary War period made for the British American Bicentennial Group Limited (owned by the Franklin Mint); a set of similar plates decorated with the state seals of the thirteen original colonies made for Colonial Williamsburg; a pillbox decorated with a cameo portrait of George Washington in pale blue, black and white made for the Churchill Mint; a Queen's Ware plate showing the North Meeting House made for the Hingham (Massachusetts) Bicentennial Commission; and a blue and white Jasper bowl decorated with portraits of George Washington, Benjamin Franklin, Thomas Jefferson, Francis Hopkinson, Ceasar Rodney and Philip Livingston made for the John Wanamaker department stores.

In an article appearing in the December 1972 issue of the *Wedgwood Review,* Claudia A. Coleman, Vice-President of Josiah Wedgwood and Sons Inc., discusses the relationship between the Wedgwood company and their American market. Citing the close ties engendered by a common language and a common ancestry, Coleman comments upon America's long-standing appreciation of English craftsmanship. She points out that the well-documented liberal political views of the company's founder, Josiah Wedgwood, are particularly significant in terms of the company's relationship with America. "The founders of the United States of America and the founder of Wedgwood were contemporaries both determined to gain their independence. In 1759 when Josiah Wedgwood took the decision to enter into business for himself, political events in America had already begun to shape toward the inevitable revolution which changed the course of that young country's destiny." With these facts in mind, Coleman goes on to articulate Wedgwood's present-day stance toward America:

> . . . it is therefore now appropriate that Wedgwood commemorates the American Bicentennial . . . to pay tribute to the men and events that gave birth to a new nation . . . As America has always been a most important market for Wedgwood, more than ever today, there is a very relevant present-day as well as historical reason that we join in the celebration of 200 astounding years and look forward to better still to come.[48]

Items made to celebrate the American Bicentennial, 1976.

Top row:

Left: *Queen's Ware Mug. Height 4 inches (10 cm.). Imprinted Wedgwood Made in England, American Independence Bicentennial 1776-1976, American Bicentennial 1976, Specially produced by Wedgwood to celebrate 200 years of American Independence and in tribute to the men and events that gave birth to a new nation in 1776, Designed by Richard Guyatt. Issued in a limited edition of 5000.*

Center: *Blue and white Jasper Independence Plate. Diameter 9 1/2 inches (24.2 cm.). Impressed Wedgwood Made in England, H R, imprinted Wedgwood Made in England, American Independence Bicentennial 1776-1976, Independence Hall, American Bicentennial 1976, Specially designed by Wedgwood . . . (as above), Produced only during the Bicentennial year, identification of the six historical scenes forming the border pattern.*

Right: *Black and white Jasper loving cup. Height 5 inches (12.8 cm.). Impressed Wedgwood Made in England M R 75, imprinted Wedgwood Made in England, American Independence Bicentennial 1776-1976, American Bicentennial 1976, Specially produced by Wedgwood . . . (as above), Designed by Richard Guyatt, Number 100 in a limited edition of 500.*

Bottom row:

Left: *Blue and white Jasper Bicentennial Plate. Diameter 8 1/8 inches (20.8 cm.). Impressed Wedgwood Made in England, imprinted Wedgwood Made in England, American Independence Bicentennial 1776-1976, American Bicentennial 1976, Specially designed by Wedgwood . . . (as above), identification of the portraits of the signers of the Declaration of Independence, which form the border decoration.*

Center: *Pill box decorated with three-color cameo of George Washington. Diameter (of cameo) 1 1/2 inches (3.7 cm.). Engraved on box: Bicentennial of American Independence, Portrait cameo by Wedgwood, Churchill Mint.*

Center: *Compact decorated with blue and white Jasper medallion, "Paul Revere's Ride." Diameter 2 3/4 inches (7 cm.). Paper label: The cameo on this Stratton Product is made by Josiah Wedgwood & Sons Ltd.*

Right: *Five-color Jasper trophy plate. Diameter 8 3/4 inches (22.3 cm.). Impressed Wedgwood Made in England A W X 75, imprinted Wedgwood Made in England, American Independence Bicentennial 1776-1976, American Bicentennial 1976, Specially designed by Wedgwood . . . (as above), Limited edition of 300, Number 228.*

Two examples of Wedgwood Queen's Ware commissioned for the Bicentennial, 1976. **Lett:** *made for Colonial Williamsburg. Diameter 9 5/8 inches (24.7 cm.).* **Right:** *made for the British American Bicentennial Group. Diameter 9 1/8 inches (23.1 cm.).*

Reverse sides of above plates showing backstamps. **Right:** *Wedgwood of Etruria & Barlaston Made in England, Approved by The Colonial Williamsburg Foundation, Colonial Williamsburg Foundation First Edition 1975, inscription explaining the history of the State Seal of North Carolina, which forms the central decoration.* **Left:** *Wedgwood of Etruria & Barlaston Made in England, British American Bicentennial Group 1776-1976, Commemorating the 200th Anniversary of the United States of America 1776-1976, inscription regarding scene from North Carolina's history illustrated on front.*

Footnotes

1 *Wedgwood Portraits and the American Revolution* (National Portrait Gallery, Smithsonian Institution, 1976), p. 122.

2 *Wedgwood Portraits and the American Revolution*, p. 122.

3 Steven A. Shapin, "The Pottery Philosophical Society, 1819-1835; an Examination of the Cultural Uses of Provincial Science," *Science Studies*, 2 (1972), p. 311.

4 Anthony Burton, *Josiah Wedgwood* (London: Andre Deutsch, 1976), pp. 24-25.

5 *Wedgwood Portraits and the American Revolution*, p. 123.

6 *Wedgwood Portraits and the American Revolution*, p. 123.

7 *Wedgwood Portraits and the American Revolution*, p. 124.

8 *Wedgwood Portraits and the American Revolution*, p. 125.

9 *Wedgwood Portraits and the American Revolution*, p. 126.

10 *Wedgwood Portraits and the American Revolution*, pp. 127-128.

11 *Wedgwood Portraits and the American Revolution*, p. 11.

12 Barbara and Graham Teller, "Wedgwood in New England," *Antiques Journal* (July 1965), p. 10.

13 Ann Finer and George Savage, *The Selected Letters of Josiah Wedgwood* (New York: Born-Hawes, 1965), p. 7.

14 Finer and Savage, *Selected Letters*, p. 9.

15 Finer and Savage, *Selected Letters*, p. 10.

16 Finer and Savage, *Selected Letters*, p. 29.

17 Finer and Savage, *Selected Letters*, p. 29.

18 Elizabeth Chellis, "Wedgwood and the American Scene," *The Eleventh Wedgwood International Seminar*, Henry Ford Museum, Dearborn, Michigan, May 5-7, 1966, p. 45.

19 Chellis, "Wedgwood and the American Scene," p. 45.

20 *Wedgwood Portraits and the American Revolution*, p. 13.

21 *Wedgwood Portraits and the American Revolution*, p. 13.

21 *Wedgwood Portraits and the American Revolution*, p. 13.

22 William Burton, *Josiah Wedgwood and His Pottery* (London: Cassell and Company, Ltd., 1922), p. 78.

23 *Wedgwood Portraits and the American Revolution*, p. 19.

24 *Wedgwood Portraits and the American Revolution*, p. 19.

25 John Brooke, *King George III* (New York: McGraw-Hill, 1972), p. 198.

26 Chellis, "Wedgwood and the American Scene," p. 49.

27 Also known as Giovanni Battista Nini.

28 Jean Gorely, "Jean Baptiste Nini, 1717-1786," *Old Wedgwood*, 1940, p. 60.

29 Louis Todd Ambler, *Benjamin Franklin: A Perspective*, Fogg Art Museum, Harvard University, Cambridge, Massachusetts, April 17-September 22, 1975, p. 78.

30 Ambler, *Benjamin Franklin*, p. 79.

31 Robin Reilly and George Savage, *Wedgwood: the Portrait Medallions* (London: Barrie & Jenkins Ltd., 1973), p. 149.

32 Reilly and Savage, *Wedgwood: the Portrait Medallions*, pp. 331-332.

33 Gilbert Chinard, editor, *Houdon in America: A Collection of Documents in the Jefferson Papers in the Library of Congress* (Baltimore: Johns Hopkins Press, 1930), p. xiv.

34 Alison Kelly, *Decorative Wedgwood in Architecture and Furniture* (New York: ᴠorn-Hawes 1965), p. 86.

35 Harry M. Buten, "Josiah Wedgwood and Benjamin Franklin," *Benjamin Franklin*, National Philatelic Museum, Philadelphia, Pennsylvania, January 15 - March 15, 1951, p. 157. It is interesting to note that the version of Wedgwood's letter given by Harry Buten differs somewhat from the version given by Finer and Savage in *Selected Letters*, page 311. Apparently the latter is a draft, while the former is the version that Franklin actually received. Another interesting point is that the nephew Wedgwood refers to is Thomas Byerley, who in his youth was the adventurous "black sheep" of the family. Byerley lived in Philadelphia from 1768 to 1775, when he returned to England and the family fold. During his stay in America Byerley was imprisoned for a time, apparently for misuse of funds collected to aid immigrant potters. For more information on Byerley, see Hensleigh Wedgwood, "Thomas Byerley: 1747-1810," *Wedgwood: Its Competitors and Imitators, 1800-1830*, Wedgwood International Seminar, Henry Ford Museum, Dearborn, Michigan, May 4-6, 1977.

36 Buten, "Josiah Wedgwood and Benjamin Franklin," p. 161.

37 Hugh Honour, *The European Vision of America*, (Cleveland, Ohio: Cleveland Museum of Art, 1975), p. 342.

38 Dale K. Graham, "Frankliniana: A Tribute to Benjamin Franklin," *Hobbies*, February 1975, p. 118.

39 Ralph M. Hower, *The Wedgwoods: Ten Generations of Potters* (privately printed, 1975), p. 39. Reprinted from the *Journal of Economic and Business History*, Vol. IV, Nos. 2 and 4, February and August, 1932.

40 Hower, *The Wedgwoods*, p. 42.

41 Hower, *The Wedgwoods*, p. 42.

42 Hower, *The Wedgwoods*, p. 45.

43 Charles L. Eastlake, *Hints on Household Taste in Furniture, Upholstery and Other Details* (New York: Dover Publications, Inc., 1969) p. 132-33. Reprint of fourth (revised) edition, as published by Longmans, Green and Company in 1878.

44 Eastlake, *Hints on Household Taste*, p. 188.

45 Margaret Brown Klapthor, *Official White House China: 1789 to the Present* (Washington D.C.: Smithsonian Institution Press, 1975), p. 140.

46 Klapthor, *Official White House China*, p. 141.

47 Mrs. Robert Coleman Taylor, *Liberty China and Queen's Ware* (Doubleday, Page & Company, 1924), p. 1.

48 C.A.C. (Claudia A. Coleman), "To Commemorate America's Bicentenary," *Wedgwood Review*, December 1972, p. 2.

WEDGWOOD
BAS-RELIEF WARE

by David Buten and Patricia Pelehach

Monographs in Wedgwood Studies, No. 2

ERHAPS the most common reaction of first-time visitors to the Buten Museum of Wedgwood is one of amazement at the fact that Wedgwood produced so many ceramics other than pale blue and white Jasper. We at the museum are not surprised by this reaction, since our basic goal is to exhibit and explain the vast range of items produced by a single factory over 200 years. The Buten Museum collection includes all periods and all styles; it is probably the largest, most comprehensive collection in the world. Upon viewing the collection it is immediately clear that blue and white Jasper is only a part of the total picture of Wedgwood production.

Because our intention is to show the large scope, we possibly shortchange the most common ornamental Wedgwood ware, dark blue and white Jasper. From the large amount of mail we receive inquiring about Wedgwood ware, we note that the pieces most often asked about are dark blue and white Jasper. The overwhelming number of these are pieces made between approximately 1890 and 1940.

Josiah Wedgwood recorded over 5000 experiments before he perfected a fine-grained stoneware ceramic body in 1774 that he named Jasper. Because of the popularity at the time of shell and stone cameos, he created the Jasper body to produce objects that were similar in appearance, but available at a substantially lower cost. Wedgwood discovered that he could place one color (generally white) on another (generally blue), fire them at the same time, and create a resultant piece that was aesthetically pleasing and extremely durable. The white decoration is known as bas-relief. Blue was the color most often used for the background, because it sold well, and the cobalt oxide used to tint the Jasper body blue was the coloring compound that was easiest to control during firing. Although it was the most uniform of Jasper colors, the blue did vary from batch to batch, and pieces in one batch would vary in color depending on their location in the kiln during firing.

There were three basic blues in the eighteenth century. One, described as slate blue, is a greyish blue that has not been duplicated since the eighteenth century. The more familiar color that has become known as "light blue" has been made from 1774 until the present. During this time the color has varied somewhat, but it is always easy to distinguish it from the other blue shades. The "dark blue" was the third blue color used by Wedgwood. It is best described as a very rich shade, timeless in its beauty and forming a particularly effective contrast with the white bas-relief. Perhaps the secret of this shade was the heavy use of red in the formula.

Dark blue Jasper was produced in both solid bodies and in Jasper Dip. "Dip" is a term used to describe the process of sandwiching layers of different colors together.

Cameos, for example, were sometimes made of three layers of differently colored Jaspers. These could be polished along the edges to show the strata. The relief subject was placed on top, and the piece was fired once only. Medallions were also done in a similar manner, but in two colors only, and the top layer was very thin. It is thought that the layering was initially done mainly for aesthetic reasons; but later on when Wedgwood was able to control his Jasper material and produce large vases, it was also a feature in reducing the overall cost of the piece. The potter would fashion a vase of white Jasper. After it reached the proper degree of dryness, it was "dipped" into blue-tinted Jasper. Then the relief was applied and the piece was fired. This resulted in a significant savings in cobalt and was so successful that most of the Jasper produced until World War II was Jasper Dip. Except for a few isolated items, all Jasper since the war has been solid.

At the beginning of the twentieth century, the firm began to produce a line of Dip pieces called "Bas-Relief Ware." This ware was described in the 1940-1950 catalogue as follows:

> Wedgwood Bas-Relief Ware—the white ornaments, made of the same Jasper body that Josiah Wedgwood invented in 1774 and largely from the models which his famous artists produced, are applied to a *vitreous stoneware* body which has previously been dipped in a Jasper clay slip.

The method was the same as that employed in making the earlier Jasper Dip; however, the body of the piece was *not* Jasper, but rather a less fine stoneware. At the same time Wedgwood also made a Jasper Dip line using the traditional Jasper body. Wedgwood never made the same designs in both Jasper Dip and Bas-Relief Ware. The Jasper body was used for the significantly more expensive pieces such as trophy plates, Dancing Hours bowls and vases, and other similar items.

It is assumed that Bas-Relief Ware was considerably less expensive than it would have been had the pieces been made from a Jasper body. The stoneware body was fired at a lower temperature (using less fuel), and could be formulated from less-refined clay. It is also possible that the stoneware body was less likely to be spoiled in the kiln and there was less waste.

Bas-Relief pieces vary in appearance from very fine to rather crude. Since the method of application of the various reliefs was the same for both Jasper Dip and Bas-Relief Ware, the variations in quality can only be explained by a difference in the quality control standards. Since Bas-Relief Ware was meant to be a comparatively inexpensive line, rejects had to be kept to a minimum and a lesser overall quality was tolerated.

Fine quality Bas-Relief pieces are difficult to distinguish from Jasper-bodied pieces. Certain shapes were, of course, used only in the Bas-Relief line, so that is one clue. The only other discernible difference can be found on large trays or other pieces in which a large amount of the white stoneware body is exposed. Here the surface is rough in appearance and almost spongy to the touch. The smooth, close-grained appearance characteristic of Jasper is missing. On Bas-Relief pieces that were intended for use, such as teapots, creamers, and cups, the interiors were glazed to facilitate the job of keeping the spongy body clean.

From the pieces of Bas-Relief Ware that have survived, it appears that dark blue was the most popular color. Pale blue, black and sage green were also available in the same shapes. The now sought-after colors of crimson, olive green and yellow were also available in Bas-Relief Ware during their short appearances. Some Bas-Relief pieces were completely coated with copper or silver, giving the ceramic pieces the appearance of metal.

In addition to the usual Bas-Relief line, two specialized lines, "Mounting Ware" and "Arms Ware," were also produced. Mounting Ware was decorated around the rim with a thin band of metal, normally electroplated nickel silver. The ceramic pieces were made with molded lines at the top (referred to as "roughing up") to aid in the attachment of the metal collars. The metal was actually stuck on with plaster of Paris.

The ubiquitous biscuit barrels are examples of Bas-Relief Mounting Ware. Biscuit barrels as well as other pieces in the Mounting Ware group were offered with white relief on either a single-color or two-color background. The latter, called "tri-color Jasper" by collectors, is eagerly sought today. Tri-color pieces were most commonly produced in dark and light blue with white relief. Although tri-color pieces currently command four to five times the price of two-color Jasper, in 1924 the initial additional charge was only 15 to 20%!

Also sought after by current collectors are pieces of Wedgwood Bas-Relief Arms Ware. These pieces, which are generally miniatures, were made to be sold in souvenir shops all over England. They were decorated with the appropriate "arms" or civic crest of the city in white relief.

The Buten Museum of Wedgwood library owns the printed 1923 price and shape book that was Harry Barnard's personal copy when he was writing his important book, *Wedgwood Chats*. The 1923 price book is the first catalogue in which the Bas-Relief line is listed. The many different sizes in which each shape was available are listed, as are the retail prices. The price list is in French, Italian, Spanish, and German as well as English. Most of the shapes in the line are illustrated.

Another major source of information about Bas-Relief Ware is the 1940-50 price book, which was compiled in 1938-39, but was virtually unused because of the interference of World War II. The copies of this catalogue owned by the Buten Museum do not have the accompanying price lists, but the Bas-Relief shapes are illustrated in a six-page section that is reproduced here. Also in the Buten Museum of Wedgwood library is an additional useful source of information, a factory price catalogue of "Mounting Ware," from about 1930. Eighty-two pieces are illustrated by actual photographs dating from about 1924.

From these three sources the following list of Bas-Relief shapes and sizes was compiled. It is important to note that the number of items available to the public was immense. A quick count shows that, with the variations listed, there were at least 625 different pieces available in *each* color. During the late 1920s when crimson, olive green and yellow were available in addition to the regular lines in two different blues, a green, and black, it would appear that over 3000 different pieces were offered for sale. Most of the shapes were available in Queen's Ware and other lines as well. The production and storage problems created by this vast selection must have been enormous. When one combines the effect of these problems with the financial crisis of the Depression, it seems practically a miracle that the Wedgwood firm survived. The survival of the company is all the more startling when one remembers that this vast selection of items was being produced in a factory founded in 1769, which had sunk ten feet over the years because of undermining of the ground beneath for coal explorations!

The list of Bas-Relief Ware attached is not complete. It is a starting point to which should be added the pieces that were not part of the "regular" line or which were introduced to and dropped from the line between price books.

ASH TRAY, SCOLLOPED

ASH TRAY, HEART

ASH TRAY, OLD HEART

ASH TRAY, SILVER

ASH TRAY, SPADE

ASH TRAY, CLUB

ASH TRAY, DIAMOND

ASH TRAY, 2394

BOWL, OPEN

PEPPER, IMPERIAL

SALT, IMPERIAL

MUSTARD, IMPERIAL

ASH TRAY, 2395

BOWL, BUTE

TEAPOT, STAND

ASH TRAY, 2396

BOWL, BREWSTER

PEPPER, TUB

MUSTARD, TUB

SALT, TUB

TOBACCO JAR, DOME

CICARETTE JAR

TOBACCO JAR, TAPER

MATCH BOX, SQUARE

PIN TRAY, OVAL

PIN TRAY, BARCLAY

LIP SALVE BOX

RING STAND

MATCH BOX, OVAL

PIN TRAY, SILVER

PIN TRAY, CEIN

TOOTH POWDER BOX

BONBON, SQUARE

MATCH BOX, CYLINDER

MATCH BOX, CEIN

TOOTH PICK, LAUREL

PUFF BOX, CEIN

PUFF BOX, UPRICHT

HAIR TIDY, UPRICHT

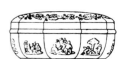
BONBON, SILVER

BONBON HEART

BONBON, PENTEFOIL

BONBON, BEAN

BONBON, SCOLLOPED

POMADE, CEIN

BONBON, ROUND

BONBON, LONC

POMADE, UPRICHT

POMADE, LAUREL

TEAPOT, 146

TEAPOT, BREWSTER

TEAPOT, ST LOUIS

SUGAR BOX, 146

SUGAR BOX, BREWSTER

SUGAR BOX, ST. LOUIS

CREAM, 146

CREAM, BREWSTER

CREAM, ST. LOUIS

CUP AND SAUCER, TEA, PEAR

CUP AND SAUCER, TEA, BREWSTER

HONEY POT, BEEHIVE

CUP AND SAUCER, TEA, BUTE, ON FOOT

CUP AND SAUCER, TEA, BUTE

CREAM, 129

CUP AND SAUCER,
COFFEE, BOSTON

CUP AND SAUCER,
COFFEE, PEAR

CUP AND SAUCER,
COFFEE, LONDON

SUGAR BOX, 129

TEA CADDY, NEW

PRESERVE JAR, UPRIGHT

BUTTER LUGGER AND STAND

COFFEE POT, 129

CANDLESTICK, BANQUET, 2139

CANDLESTICK, FLAT,

CANDLESTICK, GEIN

CANDLESTICK, READING

CANDLESTICK, PILLAR

CANDLESTICK, FLAT
WITH EXTINGUISHER

SPILL, UPRIGHT

SPILL, PERSIAN

SPILL, ACANTHUS

JUG, ORANGE

JUG, DUTCH

JUG, ETRUSCAN

JUG, BENTLEY

JUG, BYERLEY

JUG, METAL MOUNT, UPRIGHT

JUG, COVERED, UPRIGHT

JUG, UPRIGHT

BREAD AND BUTTER PLATE, NEW, SQUARE

CHEESE STAND, ROUND

BREAD AND BUTTER PLATE, ROUND

PLATE

BISCUIT JAR, STAND

BISCUIT JAR, UPRIGHT

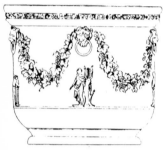

GARDEN POT, 317

MUG, UPRIGHT

COMB TRAY, OVAL

GARDEN POT, 1061

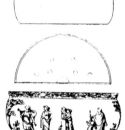

FERN DISH AND LINING, IMPERIAL

ROLL TRAY, STAR

EGG BOWL, IMPERIAL

FLOWER BASKET, 749

BOWL, SACRIFICE

COMB TRAY, SQUARE

VASE, 43

VASE, 350, WITH PLINTH

VASE, 350

VASE, 1532

VASE, 1507

VASE, 1521

VASE, 1519

VASE, 1520

VASE, 2398

VASE, 1010

VASE, 1628

VASE, 1633

POSY POT, 2389

POSY POT, 2390

POSY POT, 2391

POSY POT, 2392

POSY POT, 2393

PORTLAND VASE

VASE, 384

FERN POT, BREWSTER

FERN POT STAND,
BREWSTER

GARDEN POT AND STAND,
FLANGED

BAS-RELIEF WARE LIST

Compiled from 1923 price list, 1940 price list, and Mounting Ware catalogue in BMW library.

* pieces in 1940 list, but not in 1923 price list

** pieces appear only in mounting ware catalogue

Ashtray: Barclay, Club, Diamond*, New Heart*, Old Heart, Scalloped, Silver, Spade*, #1 (2394), #2 (2395), #3 (2396)

Beaker

Biscuit Jar (Cracker Barrel): Laurel Foot**, Upright (large, small), #1, #2, #3 (heavy decoration, slight decoration), #1672, #1673, #1674

Bowl: Brewster*, Bute*, Egg, Imperial (5 sizes), Imperial** (3 sizes), Rose**, Sacrifice

Box (Bonbon): Bean, Gein*, Heart (3 sizes), Lip Salve, Long*, Pentafoil, Puff (Upright, Brewster), Round Covered (3 sizes), Scalloped, Silver, Square, Tooth Powder (Round, Gein), #1

Butter Lugger (Tub): Lidded with stand (6 sizes), Upright** (4 sizes), #129**, #3**(heavy decoration, slight decoration)

Candlestick: Banquet*, Flat (5 sizes), Flat with extinguisher (5 sizes), Gein (4 sizes), Octagon Foot (4 sizes), Pillar (7 sizes), Reading (5 sizes), Taper (2 sizes)

Cheese Bell & Stand: Bell and stand (3 sizes), No knob on bell**

Cigarette Jar: 4½" size

Clock Case (without movement): Chippendale, Dome, Square (with or without pedestal), Tall A, Tempus Fuget, Vase Top

Comb Tray: Jersey, Oval (2 sizes), Square

Compotier: Oval, 10½" size

Drinking Horn**

Egg Cups: Single, Double

Ferndish with lining: 4 sizes

Fernpot: Brewster with matching saucer (2 sizes), Brewster with matching saucer** (2 sizes), #3** (heavy decoration)

Flower Basket: #749 (4 sizes)

Garden Pots: Flanged*, Globe (7 sizes), Imperial (8 sizes), #317 (9 sizes), #1061 (8 sizes)

Hair Tidy: D shape, Upright

Hat Pin Holder

Honey Jar: Upright**

Honey Pots: Fixed stands (4 sizes)

Inkpot & Stand: Victor

Ink Stand: Victor